Contents

Original Nestlé® Toll House® Chocolate Chip Cookies

2¼ cups all-purpose flour
1 teaspoon baking soda
1 teaspoon salt
1 cup (2 sticks) butter or margarine, softened
¾ cup granulated sugar
¾ cup packed brown sugar
1 teaspoon vanilla extract
2 large eggs
2 cups (12-ounce package) NESTLÉ TOLL HOUSE
    Semi-Sweet Chocolate Morsels
1 cup chopped nuts

PREHEAT oven to 375°F.

COMBINE flour, baking soda and salt in small bowl. Beat butter, granulated sugar, brown sugar and vanilla extract in large mixer bowl until creamy. Add eggs, one at a time, beating well after each addition. Gradually beat in flour mixture. Stir in morsels and nuts. Drop by rounded tablespoon onto ungreased baking sheets.

BAKE for 9 to 11 minutes or until golden brown. Cool on baking sheets for 2 minutes; remove to wire racks to cool completely.   *Makes about 5 dozen cookies*

Pan Cookie Variation: GREASE 15×10-inch jelly-roll pan. Prepare dough as above. Spread in prepared pan. Bake for 20 to 25 minutes or until golden brown. Cool in pan on wire rack. Makes 4 dozen bars.

COOKIES

4

Pumpkin Spiced and Iced Cookies

2¼ cups all-purpose flour
1½ teaspoons pumpkin pie spice
1 teaspoon baking powder
½ teaspoon baking soda
½ teaspoon salt
1 cup (2 sticks) butter or margarine, softened
1 cup granulated sugar
1 can (15 ounces) LIBBY'S 100% Pure Pumpkin
2 large eggs
1 teaspoon vanilla extract
2 cups (12-ounce package) NESTLÉ TOLL HOUSE
   Semi-Sweet Chocolate Morsels
1 cup chopped walnuts (optional)
   Vanilla Glaze (recipe follows)

PREHEAT oven to 375°F. Grease baking sheets.

COMBINE flour, pumpkin pie spice, baking powder, baking soda and salt in medium bowl. Beat butter and granulated sugar in large mixer bowl until creamy. Beat in pumpkin, eggs and vanilla extract. Gradually beat in flour mixture. Stir in morsels and nuts. Drop by rounded tablespoon onto prepared baking sheets.

BAKE for 15 to 20 minutes or until edges are lightly browned. Cool on baking sheets for 2 minutes; remove to wire racks to cool completely. Spread or drizzle with Vanilla Glaze.

Makes about 5½ dozen cookies

Vanilla Glaze: COMBINE 1 cup powdered sugar, 1 to 1½ tablespoons milk and ½ teaspoon vanilla extract in small bowl; mix well.

COOKIES

Island Cookies

1⅔ cups all-purpose flour
¾ teaspoon baking powder
½ teaspoon baking soda
½ teaspoon salt
¾ cup (1½ sticks) butter, softened
¾ cup packed brown sugar
⅓ cup granulated sugar
1 teaspoon vanilla extract
1 large egg
1¾ cups (11.5-ounce package) NESTLÉ TOLL HOUSE
    Milk Chocolate Morsels
1 cup flaked coconut, toasted, if desired
1 cup chopped walnuts

PREHEAT oven to 375°F.

COMBINE flour, baking powder, baking soda and salt in small bowl. Beat butter, brown sugar, granulated sugar and vanilla extract in large mixer bowl until creamy. Beat in egg. Gradually beat in flour mixture. Stir in morsels, coconut and nuts. Drop by slightly rounded tablespoon onto ungreased baking sheets.

BAKE for 8 to 11 minutes or until edges are lightly browned. Cool on baking sheets for 2 minutes; remove to wire racks to cool completely.   *Makes about 3 dozen cookies*

Note: NESTLÉ TOLL HOUSE Semi-Sweet Chocolate Morsels, Semi-Sweet Chocolate Mini Morsels, Premier White Morsels or Butterscotch Flavored Morsels can be substituted for the Milk Chocolate Morsels.

COOKIES

Mini Chip Snowball Cookies

1½ cups (3 sticks) butter or margarine, softened
¾ cup powdered sugar
1 tablespoon vanilla extract
½ teaspoon salt
3 cups all-purpose flour
2 cups (12-ounce package) NESTLÉ TOLL HOUSE
   Semi-Sweet Chocolate Mini Morsels
½ cup finely chopped nuts
   Powdered sugar

PREHEAT oven to 375°F.

BEAT butter, sugar, vanilla extract and salt in large mixer bowl until creamy. Gradually beat in flour; stir in morsels and nuts. Shape level tablespoons of dough into 1¼-inch balls. Place on ungreased baking sheets.

BAKE for 10 to 12 minutes or until cookies are set and lightly browned. Remove from oven. Sift powdered sugar over hot cookies on baking sheets. Cool on baking sheets for 10 minutes; remove to wire racks to cool completely. Sprinkle with additional powdered sugar, if desired. Store in airtight containers.

Makes about 5 dozen cookies

COOKIES

7

Chocolate Chip Shells

2 cups all-purpose flour
1⅓ cups (about 8 ounces) NESTLÉ TOLL HOUSE Semi-Sweet
  Chocolate Morsels, *divided*
4 large eggs
1 cup granulated sugar
1 tablespoon orange liqueur (such as Cointreau) *or*
  1 teaspoon orange extract
1 teaspoon vanilla extract
2 tablespoons (about 1 orange) grated orange peel
1 cup (2 sticks) unsalted butter, melted
Sifted powdered sugar

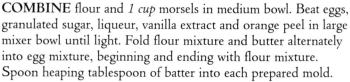

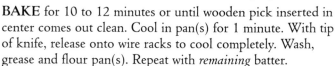

PREHEAT oven to 350°F. Generously grease and flour madeleine baking pan(s).

COMBINE flour and *1 cup* morsels in medium bowl. Beat eggs, granulated sugar, liqueur, vanilla extract and orange peel in large mixer bowl until light. Fold flour mixture and butter alternately into egg mixture, beginning and ending with flour mixture. Spoon heaping tablespoon of batter into each prepared mold.

BAKE for 10 to 12 minutes or until wooden pick inserted in center comes out clean. Cool in pan(s) for 1 minute. With tip of knife, release onto wire racks to cool completely. Wash, grease and flour pan(s). Repeat with *remaining* batter.

SPRINKLE madeleines very lightly with powdered sugar. Microwave *remaining* morsels in *heavy-duty* resealable plastic food storage bag on HIGH (100%) power for 30 seconds; knead bag. Microwave at additional 10-second intervals, kneading until smooth. Cut small hole in corner of bag; squeeze to drizzle over madeleines. Allow chocolate to cool and set before serving.

Makes about 2½ dozen madeleines

COOKIES

Jumbo 3-Chip Cookies

4 cups all-purpose flour
1 teaspoon baking powder
1 teaspoon baking soda
1½ cups (3 sticks) butter, softened
1¼ cups granulated sugar
1¼ cups packed brown sugar
2 large eggs
1 tablespoon vanilla extract
1 cup (6 ounces) NESTLÉ TOLL HOUSE Milk Chocolate Morsels
1 cup (6 ounces) NESTLÉ TOLL HOUSE Semi-Sweet Chocolate Morsels
½ cup NESTLÉ TOLL HOUSE Premier White Morsels
1 cup chopped nuts

PREHEAT oven to 375°F.

COMBINE flour, baking powder and baking soda in medium bowl. Beat butter, granulated sugar and brown sugar in large mixer bowl until creamy. Beat in eggs and vanilla extract. Gradually beat in flour mixture. Stir in morsels and nuts. Drop dough by level ¼ cup measure 2 inches apart onto ungreased baking sheets.

BAKE for 12 to 14 minutes or until light golden brown. Cool on baking sheets for 2 minutes; remove to wire racks to cool completely.   *Makes about 2 dozen cookies*

COOKIES

9

Chunky Chocolate Chip Peanut Butter Cookies

1¼ cups all-purpose flour
½ teaspoon baking soda
½ teaspoon salt
½ teaspoon ground cinnamon
¾ cup (1½ sticks) butter or margarine, softened
½ cup granulated sugar
½ cup packed brown sugar
½ cup creamy peanut butter
1 large egg
1 teaspoon vanilla extract
2 cups (12-ounce package) NESTLÉ TOLL HOUSE
  Semi-Sweet Chocolate Morsels
½ cup coarsely chopped peanuts

PREHEAT oven to 375°F.

COMBINE flour, baking soda, salt and cinnamon in small bowl. Beat butter, granulated sugar, brown sugar and peanut butter in large mixer bowl until creamy. Beat in egg and vanilla extract. Gradually beat in flour mixture. Stir in morsels and peanuts.

DROP dough by rounded tablespoon onto ungreased baking sheets. Press down slightly to flatten into 2-inch circles.

BAKE for 7 to 10 minutes or until edges are set but centers are still soft. Cool on baking sheets for 4 minutes; remove to wire racks to cool completely.   *Makes about 3 dozen cookies*

COOKIES

Oatmeal Scotchies

1¼ cups all-purpose flour
1 teaspoon baking soda
½ teaspoon salt
½ teaspoon ground cinnamon
1 cup (2 sticks) butter or margarine, softened
¾ cup granulated sugar
¾ cup packed brown sugar
2 large eggs
1 teaspoon vanilla extract *or* grated peel of 1 orange
3 cups quick or old-fashioned oats
1⅔ cups (11-ounce package) NESTLÉ TOLL HOUSE Butterscotch Flavored Morsels

PREHEAT oven to 375°F.

COMBINE flour, baking soda, salt and cinnamon in small bowl. Beat butter, granulated sugar, brown sugar, eggs and vanilla extract in large mixer bowl. Gradually beat in flour mixture. Stir in oats and morsels. Drop by rounded tablespoon onto ungreased baking sheets.

BAKE for 7 to 8 minutes for chewy cookies or 9 to 10 minutes for crispy cookies. Cool on baking sheets for 2 minutes; remove to wire racks to cool completely.

Makes about 4 dozen cookies

Pan Cookie Variation: GREASE 15×10-inch jelly-roll pan. Spread dough into prepared pan. Bake for 18 to 22 minutes or until light brown. Cool completely in pan on wire rack. Makes 4 dozen bars.

COOKIES

11

Milk Chocolate Florentine Cookies

⅔ cup butter
2 cups quick oats
1 cup granulated sugar
⅔ cup all-purpose flour
¼ cup light or dark corn syrup
¼ cup milk
1 teaspoon vanilla extract
¼ teaspoon salt
1¾ cups (11.5-ounce package) NESTLÉ TOLL HOUSE Milk Chocolate Morsels

PREHEAT oven to 375°F. Line baking sheets with foil.

MELT butter in medium saucepan; remove from heat. Stir in oats, sugar, flour, corn syrup, milk, vanilla extract and salt; mix well. Drop by level teaspoon, about 3 inches apart, onto prepared baking sheets. Spread thinly with rubber spatula.

BAKE for 6 to 8 minutes or until golden brown. Cool completely on baking sheets on wire racks. Peel foil from cookies.

MICROWAVE morsels in medium, uncovered, microwave-safe bowl on MEDIUM-HIGH (70%) power for 1 minute. STIR. Morsels may retain some of their original shape. If necessary, microwave at additional 10- to 15-second intervals, stirring just until morsels are melted. Spread thin layer of melted chocolate onto flat side of *half* the cookies. Top with *remaining* cookies.

Makes about 3½ dozen sandwich cookies

COOKIES

Chocolatey Raspberry Crumb Bars

1 cup (2 sticks) butter or margarine, softened
2 cups all-purpose flour
½ cup packed light brown sugar
¼ teaspoon salt
2 cups (12-ounce package) NESTLÉ TOLL HOUSE
  Semi-Sweet Chocolate Morsels, *divided*
1 can (14 ounces) NESTLÉ CARNATION Sweetened
  Condensed Milk
½ cup chopped nuts (optional)
⅓ cup seedless raspberry jam

PREHEAT oven to 350°F. Grease 13×9-inch baking pan.

BEAT butter in large mixer bowl until creamy. Beat in flour, sugar and salt until crumbly. With floured fingers, press 1¾ *cups* crumb mixture onto bottom of prepared baking pan; reserve *remaining* mixture.

BAKE for 10 to 12 minutes or until edges are golden brown.

MICROWAVE *1 cup* morsels and condensed milk in medium, uncovered, microwave-safe bowl on HIGH (100%) power for 1 minute. STIR. Morsels may retain some of their original shape. If necessary, microwave at additional 10- to 15-second intervals, stirring just until morsels are melted. Spread over hot crust.

STIR nuts into *reserved* crumb mixture; sprinkle over chocolate layer. Drop teaspoonfuls of raspberry jam over crumb mixture. Sprinkle with *remaining* morsels.

BAKE for 25 to 30 minutes or until center is set. Cool in pan on wire rack. Cut into bars.   *Makes 3 dozen bars*

BAR COOKIES

13

White Chip Meringue Dessert Bars

Crust

    2 cups all-purpose flour
    ½ cup powdered sugar
    1 cup (2 sticks) butter or margarine, softened

Topping

    2 cups (12-ounce package) NESTLÉ TOLL HOUSE
        Premier White Morsels
  1¼ cups coarsely chopped nuts, *divided*
    3 large egg whites
    1 cup packed brown sugar

PREHEAT oven to 375°F.

For Crust

COMBINE flour and powdered sugar in medium bowl. Cut in butter with pastry blender or 2 knives until mixture is crumbly. Press evenly onto bottom of ungreased 13×9-inch baking pan.

BAKE for 10 to 12 minutes or until set.

For Topping

SPRINKLE morsels and *1 cup* nuts over hot crust. Beat egg whites in small mixer bowl until frothy. Gradually add brown sugar. Beat until stiff peaks form. Carefully spread meringue over morsels and nuts. Sprinkle with *remaining* nuts.

BAKE for 15 to 20 minutes or until golden brown. Serve warm or cool completely. Cut into bars.   *Makes about 2 dozen bars*

BAR COOKIES

No-Bake Chocolate Peanut Butter Bars

2 cups peanut butter, *divided*
¾ cup (1½ sticks) butter, softened
2 cups powdered sugar
3 cups graham cracker crumbs
2 cups (12-ounce package) NESTLÉ TOLL HOUSE
Semi-Sweet Chocolate Mini Morsels, *divided*

GREASE 13×9-inch baking pan.

BEAT *1¼* cups peanut butter and butter in large mixer bowl until creamy. Gradually beat in *1 cup* powdered sugar. With hands or wooden spoon, work in *remaining* powdered sugar, graham cracker crumbs and *½ cup* morsels. Press evenly into prepared pan. Smooth top with spatula.

MELT *remaining* peanut butter and *remaining* morsels in medium, *heavy-duty* saucepan over *lowest possible heat*, stirring constantly, until smooth. Spread over graham cracker crust in pan. Refrigerate for at least 1 hour or until chocolate is firm; cut into bars. Store in refrigerator.   *Makes 5 dozen bars*

Easy Double Chocolate Chip Brownies

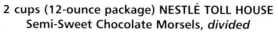

2 cups (12-ounce package) NESTLÉ TOLL HOUSE
   Semi-Sweet Chocolate Morsels, *divided*
½ cup (1 stick) butter or margarine, cut into pieces
3 large eggs
1¼ cups all-purpose flour
1 cup granulated sugar
1 teaspoon vanilla extract
¼ teaspoon baking soda
½ cup chopped nuts

PREHEAT oven to 350°F. Grease 13×9-inch baking pan.

MELT *1 cup* morsels and butter in large, *heavy-duty* saucepan over low heat; stir until smooth. Remove from heat. Stir in eggs. Stir in flour, sugar, vanilla extract and baking soda. Stir in *remaining* morsels and nuts. Spread into prepared baking pan.

BAKE for 18 to 22 minutes or until wooden pick inserted in center comes out slightly sticky. Cool completely in pan on wire rack. Cut into bars.   *Makes 2 dozen brownies*

BAR COOKIES

Razz-Ma-Tazz Bars

½ cup (1 stick) butter or margarine
2 cups (12-ounce package) NESTLÉ TOLL HOUSE
    Premier White Morsels, *divided*
2 large eggs
½ cup granulated sugar
1 cup all-purpose flour
½ teaspoon salt
½ teaspoon almond extract
½ cup seedless raspberry jam
¼ cup toasted sliced almonds

PREHEAT oven to 325°F. Grease and sugar 9-inch square baking pan.

MELT butter in medium, uncovered, microwave-safe bowl on HIGH (100%) power for 1 minute; stir. Add *1 cup* morsels; let stand. Do not stir.

BEAT eggs in large mixer bowl until foamy. Add sugar; beat until light lemon colored, about 5 minutes. Stir in morsel-butter mixture. Add flour, salt and almond extract; mix at low speed until combined. Spread ⅔ of batter into prepared pan.

BAKE for 15 to 17 minutes or until light golden brown around edges. Remove from oven to wire rack.

HEAT jam in small, microwave-safe bowl on HIGH (100%) power for 30 seconds; stir. Spread jam over warm crust. Stir *remaining* morsels into *remaining* batter. Drop spoonfuls of batter over jam. Sprinkle with almonds.

BAKE for 25 to 30 minutes or until edges are browned. Cool completely in pan on wire rack. Cut into bars.

Makes 16 bars

**BAR
COOKIES**

17

Rocky Road Bars

2 cups (12-ounce package) NESTLÉ TOLL HOUSE
   Semi-Sweet Chocolate Morsels, *divided*
1½ cups all-purpose flour
1½ teaspoons baking powder
   1 cup granulated sugar
   6 tablespoons (¾ stick) butter or margarine, softened
1½ teaspoons vanilla extract
   2 large eggs
   2 cups miniature marshmallows
1½ cups coarsely chopped walnuts

PREHEAT oven to 375°F. Grease 13×9-inch baking pan.

MICROWAVE *1 cup* morsels in medium, uncovered, microwave-safe bowl on HIGH (100%) power for 1 minute. STIR. Morsels may retain some of their original shape. If necessary, microwave at additional 10- to 15-second intervals, stirring just until morsels are melted. Cool to room temperature. Combine flour and baking powder in small bowl.

BEAT sugar, butter and vanilla in large mixer bowl until crumbly. Beat in eggs. Add melted chocolate; beat until smooth. Gradually beat in flour mixture. Spread batter into prepared baking pan.

BAKE for 16 to 20 minutes or until wooden pick inserted in center comes out slightly sticky.

REMOVE from oven; sprinkle immediately with marshmallows, nuts and *remaining* morsels. Return to oven for 2 minutes or just until marshmallows begin to melt. Cool in pan on wire rack for 20 to 30 minutes. Cut into bars with wet knife. Serve warm.

Makes 2½ dozen bars

Caramel Oatmeal Chewies

1¾ cups quick or old-fashioned oats
1¾ cups all-purpose flour, *divided*
 ¾ cup packed brown sugar
 ½ teaspoon baking soda
 ¼ teaspoon salt (optional)
 ¾ cup (1½ sticks) butter or margarine, melted
 2 cups (12-ounce package) NESTLÉ TOLL HOUSE
    Semi-Sweet Chocolate Morsels
 1 cup chopped nuts
 1 cup caramel ice cream topping

PREHEAT oven to 350°F. Grease bottom of 13×9-inch baking pan.

COMBINE oats, *1½ cups* flour, brown sugar, baking soda and salt in large bowl. Stir in butter; mix well. Reserve *1 cup* oat mixture; press *remaining* oat mixture onto bottom of prepared baking pan.

BAKE for 12 to 15 minutes or until golden brown. Sprinkle with morsels and nuts. Mix caramel topping with *remaining* flour in small bowl; drizzle over morsels to within ¼ inch of pan edges. Sprinkle with *reserved* oat mixture.

BAKE for 18 to 22 minutes or until golden brown. Cool in pan on wire rack; refrigerate until firm.

Makes about 2½ dozen bars

BAR COOKIES

19

Layers of Love
Chocolate Brownies

¾ cup all-purpose flour
¾ cup NESTLÉ TOLL HOUSE Baking Cocoa
¼ teaspoon salt
½ cup (1 stick) butter, cut in pieces
½ cup granulated sugar
½ cup packed brown sugar
3 large eggs, *divided*
2 teaspoons vanilla extract
1 cup chopped pecans
¾ cup NESTLÉ TOLL HOUSE Premier White Morsels
½ cup caramel ice cream topping
¾ cup NESTLÉ TOLL HOUSE Semi-Sweet Chocolate Morsels

PREHEAT oven to 350°F. Grease 8-inch square baking pan.

COMBINE flour, cocoa and salt in small bowl. Beat butter, granulated sugar and brown sugar in large mixer bowl until creamy. Add *2 eggs*, one at a time, beating well after each addition. Add vanilla extract; mix well. Gradually beat in flour mixture. Reserve *¾ cup* batter. Spread *remaining* batter into prepared baking pan. Sprinkle pecans and white morsels over batter. Drizzle caramel topping over top. Beat *remaining* egg and *reserved* batter in same large bowl until light in color. Stir in semi-sweet morsels. Spread evenly over caramel topping.

BAKE for 30 to 35 minutes or until center is set. Cool completely in pan on wire rack. Cut into squares.

Makes 16 brownies

BAR COOKIES

Swirled Peanut Butter Chocolate Cheesecake Bars

Crust
   2 cups graham cracker crumbs
   ½ cup (1 stick) butter or margarine, melted
   ⅓ cup granulated sugar

Filling
   2 packages (8 ounces *each*) cream cheese, softened
   1 cup granulated sugar
   ¼ cup all-purpose flour
   1 can (12 fluid ounces) NESTLÉ CARNATION Evaporated Milk
   2 large eggs
   1 tablespoon vanilla extract
   1 cup (6 ounces) NESTLÉ TOLL HOUSE Peanut Butter &
      Milk Chocolate Morsels

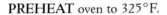

PREHEAT oven to 325°F.

For Crust

COMBINE graham cracker crumbs, butter and sugar in medium bowl; press onto bottom of ungreased 13×9-inch baking pan.

For Filling

BEAT cream cheese, sugar and flour in large mixer bowl until smooth. Gradually beat in evaporated milk, eggs and vanilla extract.

MICROWAVE morsels in medium, uncovered, microwave-safe bowl on MEDIUM-HIGH (70%) power for 1 minute. STIR. Morsels may retain some of their original shape. If necessary, microwave at additional 10- to 15-second intervals, stirring just until morsels are melted. Stir *1 cup* cream cheese mixture into chocolate. Pour *remaining* cream cheese mixture over crust. Pour chocolate mixture over cream cheese mixture. Swirl mixtures with spoon, pulling plain cream cheese mixture up to surface.

BAKE for 40 to 45 minutes or until set. Cool completely in pan on wire rack; refrigerate until firm. Cut into bars.

Makes 15 bars

BAR COOKIES

Chunky Pecan Pie Bars

Crust

1½ cups all-purpose flour
½ cup (1 stick) butter or margarine, softened
¼ cup packed brown sugar

Filling
3 large eggs
¾ cup corn syrup
¾ cup granulated sugar
2 tablespoons butter or margarine, melted
1 teaspoon vanilla extract
1¾ cups (11.5-ounce package) NESTLÉ TOLL HOUSE
    Semi-Sweet Chocolate Chunks
1½ cups coarsely chopped pecans

PREHEAT oven to 350°F. Grease 13×9-inch baking pan.

For Crust

BEAT flour, butter and brown sugar in small mixer bowl until crumbly. Press into prepared baking pan.

BAKE for 12 to 15 minutes or until lightly browned.

For Filling

BEAT eggs, corn syrup, granulated sugar, butter and vanilla extract in medium bowl with wire whisk. Stir in chunks and nuts. Pour evenly over baked crust.

BAKE for 25 to 30 minutes or until set. Cool completely in pan on wire rack. Cut into bars.   *Makes 2 to 3 dozen bars*

BAR COOKIES

Premier Cheesecake Cranberry Bars

2 cups all-purpose flour
1½ cups quick or old-fashioned oats
¼ cup packed light brown sugar
1 cup (2 sticks) butter or margarine, softened
2 cups (12-ounce package) NESTLÉ TOLL HOUSE Premier White Morsels
1 package (8 ounces) cream cheese, softened
1 can (14 ounces) NESTLÉ CARNATION Sweetened Condensed Milk
¼ cup lemon juice
1 teaspoon vanilla extract
1 can (16 ounces) whole-berry cranberry sauce
2 tablespoons cornstarch

PREHEAT oven to 350°F. Grease 13×9-inch baking pan.

COMBINE flour, oats and brown sugar in large bowl. Add butter; mix until crumbly. Stir in morsels. Reserve *2½ cups* morsel mixture for topping. With floured fingers, press *remaining* mixture into prepared pan.

BEAT cream cheese in large mixer bowl until creamy. Add sweetened condensed milk, lemon juice and vanilla extract; mix until smooth. Pour over crust. Combine cranberry sauce and cornstarch in medium bowl. Spoon over cream cheese mixture. Sprinkle *reserved* morsel mixture over cranberry mixture.

BAKE for 35 to 40 minutes or until center is set. Cool completely in pan on wire rack. Cover; refrigerate until serving time (up to 1 day). Cut into bars. *Makes 2½ dozen bars*

BAR COOKIES

Peanutty Gooey Bars

Crust

    2 cups chocolate graham cracker crumbs
    ½ cup (1 stick) butter or margarine, melted
    ⅓ cup granulated sugar

Topping

    1⅔ cups (11-ounce package) NESTLÉ TOLL HOUSE Peanut
        Butter & Milk Chocolate Morsels, *divided*
    1 can (14 ounces) NESTLÉ CARNATION Sweetened
        Condensed Milk
    1 teaspoon vanilla extract
    1 cup coarsely chopped peanuts

PREHEAT oven to 350°F.

For Crust

COMBINE graham cracker crumbs, butter and sugar in medium bowl; press onto bottom of ungreased 13×9-inch baking pan.

For Topping

MICROWAVE *1 cup* morsels, sweetened condensed milk and vanilla extract in medium, uncovered, microwave-safe bowl on HIGH (100%) power for 1 minute. STIR. Morsels may retain some of their original shape. If necessary, microwave at additional 10- to 15-second intervals, stirring until morsels are melted. Pour evenly over crust. Top with nuts and *remaining* morsels.

BAKE for 20 to 25 minutes or until edges are bubbly. Cool completely in pan on wire rack. Cut into bars.

Makes 2 dozen bars

**BAR
COOKIES**

Chocolate Chip Cheesecake

Crust

1½ cups (about 15) crushed chocolate sandwich cookies
2 tablespoons butter or margarine, melted
2 cups (12-ounce package) NESTLÉ TOLL HOUSE
   Semi-Sweet Chocolate Mini Morsels, *divided*

Filling

2 packages (8 ounces *each*) cream cheese, softened
½ cup granulated sugar
1 tablespoon vanilla extract
2 large eggs
2 tablespoons all-purpose flour
¾ cup NESTLÉ CARNATION Evaporated Milk
½ cup sour cream

PREHEAT oven to 300°F.

For Crust

COMBINE cookie crumbs and butter in medium bowl until moistened; press onto bottom of ungreased 9-inch springform pan. Sprinkle with *1 cup* morsels.

For Filling

BEAT cream cheese, sugar and vanilla extract in large mixer bowl until smooth. Beat in eggs and flour. Gradually beat in evaporated milk and sour cream. Pour over crust. Sprinkle with *remaining* morsels.

BAKE for 25 minutes. Cover loosely with aluminum foil. Bake for additional 30 to 40 minutes or until edge is set but center still moves slightly. Place in refrigerator immediately; refrigerate for 2 hours or until firm. Remove side of springform pan.

Makes 12 to 14 servings

CAKES

Rich Chocolate Cake with Creamy Peanut Butter Milk Chocolate Frosting

Cake

     2 cups all-purpose flour
     1¾ cups granulated sugar
     ⅔ cup NESTLÉ TOLL HOUSE Baking Cocoa
     1½ teaspoons baking powder
     1½ teaspoons baking soda
     ½ teaspoon salt
     1 cup milk
     1 cup water
     ½ cup vegetable oil
     2 large eggs
     2 teaspoons vanilla extract
     1⅔ cups (11-ounce package) NESTLÉ TOLL HOUSE
          Peanut Butter & Milk Chocolate Morsels, *divided*

Creamy Peanut Butter Milk Chocolate Frosting

     1 package (8 ounces) cream cheese, softened
     1 teaspoon vanilla extract
     ⅛ teaspoon salt
     3 cups powdered sugar

Garnish

     1 bar (2 ounces *total*) NESTLÉ TOLL HOUSE Semi-Sweet
          Chocolate Baking Bar, made into curls (see Tip)

PREHEAT oven to 350°F. Grease and flour two 9-inch-round cake pans.

For Cake

COMBINE flour, granulated sugar, cocoa, baking powder, baking soda and salt in large mixer bowl. Add milk, water, vegetable oil, eggs and vanilla extract; blend until moistened. Beat for 2 minutes (batter will be thin). Pour into prepared pans. Sprinkle ⅓ *cup* morsels over each cake layer.

CAKES

BAKE for 25 to 30 minutes or until wooden pick inserted in center comes out clean. Cool in pans on wire racks for 10 minutes; remove to wire racks to cool completely. Frost with Creamy Peanut Butter Milk Chocolate Frosting between layers and on top and side of cake. Garnish with chocolate curls before serving.

For Creamy Peanut Butter Milk Chocolate Frosting

MICROWAVE *remaining* morsels in small, uncovered, microwave-safe bowl on MEDIUM-HIGH (70%) power for 1 minute. STIR. Morsels may retain some of their original shape. If necessary, microwave at additional 10- to 15-second intervals, stirring just until morsels are melted. Beat cream cheese, melted morsels, vanilla extract and salt in small mixer bowl until light and fluffy. Gradually beat in powdered sugar.

Makes 10 to 12 servings

Tip: To make chocolate curls, carefully draw a vegetable peeler across a bar of NESTLÉ TOLL HOUSE Semi-Sweet Chocolate. Vary the width of your curls by using different sides of the chocolate bar.

CAKES

Chocolate Intensity

Cake

    4 bars (8-ounce box) NESTLÉ TOLL HOUSE Unsweetened
        Chocolate Baking Bars, broken into pieces
  1½ cups granulated sugar
   ½ cup (1 stick) butter, softened
   3 large eggs
   2 teaspoons vanilla extract
   ⅔ cup all-purpose flour

Coffee Crème Anglaise Sauce

   ⅓ cup granulated sugar
   1 tablespoon TASTER'S CHOICE 100% Pure Instant Coffee
  1½ cups milk
   4 large egg yolks, lightly beaten
   1 teaspoon vanilla extract

PREHEAT oven to 350°F. Grease 9-inch springform pan.

For Cake

MICROWAVE baking bars in medium microwave-safe bowl on HIGH (100%) power for 1 minute. STIR. Bars may retain some of original shape. If necessary, microwave at additional 10-to 15-second intervals, stirring until smooth. Cool to lukewarm.

BEAT sugar, butter, eggs and vanilla extract in small bowl for about 4 minutes or until thick and pale yellow. Beat in melted chocolate. Gradually beat in flour. Spread into springform pan.

BAKE for 25 to 28 minutes or until wooden pick inserted in center comes out moist. Cool in pan on wire rack for 15 minutes. Loosen and remove side of pan; cool completely. Sprinkle with powdered sugar; serve with Coffee Crème Anglaise Sauce.

For Coffee Crème Anglaise Sauce

COMBINE sugar and Taster's Choice in medium saucepan; stir in milk. Cook over medium heat, stirring constantly, until mixture comes just to a very gentle boil. Remove from heat. Gradually whisk *half* of hot milk mixture into egg yolks; return mixture to saucepan. Cook, stirring constantly, for 3 to 4 minutes or until slightly thickened. Strain into small bowl; stir in vanilla extract. Cover; refrigerate. *Makes 10 to 12 servings*

CAKES

Zesty Lemon Pound Cake

1 cup (6 ounces) NESTLÉ TOLL HOUSE Premier White
   Morsels *or* 3 bars (6-ounce box) NESTLÉ TOLL HOUSE
   Premier White Baking Bars, broken into pieces
2½ cups all-purpose flour
1 teaspoon baking powder
½ teaspoon salt
1 cup (2 sticks) butter, softened
1½ cups granulated sugar
2 teaspoons vanilla extract
3 large eggs
3 to 4 tablespoons grated lemon peel (about 3 lemons)
1⅓ cups buttermilk
1 cup powdered sugar
3 tablespoons fresh lemon juice

PREHEAT oven to 350°F. Grease and flour 12-cup Bundt pan.

MELT morsels in medium, uncovered, microwave-safe bowl on
MEDIUM-HIGH (70%) power for 1 minute. STIR. Morsels
may retain some of their original shape. If necessary, microwave
at additional 10- to 15-second intervals, stirring just until
morsels are melted. Cool slightly.

COMBINE flour, baking powder and salt in small bowl. Beat
butter, granulated sugar and vanilla in large mixer bowl until
creamy. Beat in eggs, one at a time, beating well after each addition.
Beat in lemon peel and melted morsels. Gradually beat in flour
mixture alternately with buttermilk. Pour into prepared pan.

BAKE for 50 to 55 minutes or until wooden pick inserted in
cake comes out clean. Cool in pan on wire rack for 10 minutes.
Combine powdered sugar and lemon juice in small bowl. Make
holes in cake with wooden pick; pour *half* of lemon glaze over
cake. Let stand for 5 minutes. Invert onto plate. Make holes in
top of cake; pour *remaining* glaze over cake. Cool completely
before serving. *Makes 16 servings*

CAKES

Triple Chip Cheesecake

Crust
1¾ cups chocolate graham cracker crumbs
⅓ cup butter or margarine, melted

Filling
3 packages (8 ounces *each*) cream cheese, softened
¾ cup granulated sugar
½ cup sour cream
3 tablespoons all-purpose flour
1½ teaspoons vanilla extract
3 large eggs
1 cup (6 ounces) NESTLÉ TOLL HOUSE Butterscotch
    Flavored Morsels
1 cup (6 ounces) NESTLÉ TOLL HOUSE Semi-Sweet
    Chocolate Morsels
1 cup (6 ounces) NESTLÉ TOLL HOUSE Premier
    White Morsels

Topping
1 tablespoon *each* NESTLÉ TOLL HOUSE Butterscotch
    Flavored Morsels, Semi-Sweet Chocolate Morsels
    and Premier White Morsels

PREHEAT oven to 300°F. Grease 9-inch springform pan.

For Crust

COMBINE crumbs and butter in small bowl. Press onto bottom and 1 inch up side of prepared pan.

For Filling

BEAT cream cheese and granulated sugar in large mixer bowl until smooth. Add sour cream, flour and vanilla extract; mix well. Add eggs; beat on low speed until combined.

MELT butterscotch morsels according to package directions. Stir until smooth. Add *1½ cups* batter to melted morsels. Pour into crust. Repeat procedure with semi-sweet morsels. Carefully spoon over butterscotch layer. Melt Premier White morsels according to package directions and blend into *remaining* batter in mixer bowl. Carefully pour over semi-sweet layer.

CAKES

BAKE for 1 hour and 10 to 15 minutes or until center is almost set. Cool in pan on wire rack for 10 minutes. Run knife around edge of cheesecake. Let stand for 1 hour.

For Topping

PLACE each flavor of morsels separately into three small, *heavy-duty* resealable plastic food storage bags. Microwave on HIGH (100%) power for 20 seconds; knead bags to mix. Microwave at additional 10-second intervals, kneading until smooth. Cut small hole in corner of each bag; squeeze to drizzle over cheesecake. Refrigerate for at least 3 hours or overnight. Remove side of pan.

Makes 12 to 16 servings

CAKES

Toll House® Crumbcake

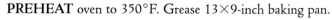

Topping

- ⅓ cup packed brown sugar
- 1 tablespoon all-purpose flour
- 2 tablespoons butter or margarine, softened
- ½ cup chopped nuts
- 2 cups (12-ounce package) NESTLÉ TOLL HOUSE Semi-Sweet Chocolate Mini Morsels, *divided*

Cake

- 1¾ cups all-purpose flour
- 1 teaspoon baking powder
- 1 teaspoon baking soda
- ¼ teaspoon salt
- ¾ cup granulated sugar
- ½ cup (1 stick) butter or margarine, softened
- 1 teaspoon vanilla extract
- 3 large eggs
- 1 cup sour cream

PREHEAT oven to 350°F. Grease 13×9-inch baking pan.

For Topping

COMBINE brown sugar, flour and butter in small bowl with pastry blender or two knives until crumbly. Stir in nuts and *½ cup* morsels.

For Cake

COMBINE flour, baking powder, baking soda and salt in small bowl. Beat granulated sugar, butter and vanilla extract in large mixer bowl until creamy. Add eggs, one at a time, beating well after each addition. Gradually add flour mixture alternately with sour cream. Fold in *remaining 1½ cups* morsels. Spread into prepared baking pan; sprinkle with topping.

BAKE for 25 to 35 minutes or until wooden pick inserted in center comes out clean. Cool in pan on wire rack.

Makes 12 servings

CAKES

Strawberry Cheesecake Pie

1 *prepared* 9-inch (6 ounces) graham cracker crumb crust
⅔ cup (5-fluid-ounce can) NESTLÉ CARNATION Evaporated
    Fat Free Milk
1 package (8 ounces) fat-free cream cheese, softened
1 egg
½ cup granulated sugar
2 tablespoons all-purpose flour
1 teaspoon grated lemon peel
1½ to 2 cups halved fresh strawberries
3 tablespoons strawberry jelly, warmed

PREHEAT oven to 325°F.

PLACE evaporated milk, cream cheese, egg, sugar, flour and
lemon peel in blender; cover. Blend until smooth. Pour into
crust.

BAKE for 35 to 40 minutes or until center is set. Cool
completely in pan on wire rack. Arrange strawberries on
top of pie; drizzle with jelly. Refrigerate well before serving.

Makes 8 servings

PIES

33

Easy Coconut Banana Cream Pie

1 *prebaked* 9-inch (4-cup volume) deep-dish pie shell
1 can (14 ounces) NESTLÉ CARNATION Sweetened
   Condensed Milk
1 cup cold water
1 package (3.4 ounces) vanilla or banana cream instant
   pudding and pie filling mix
1 cup flaked coconut
1 container (8 ounces) frozen whipped topping, thawed,
   divided
2 medium bananas, sliced, dipped in lemon juice
   Toasted or tinted flaked coconut (optional)

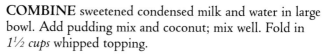

COMBINE sweetened condensed milk and water in large bowl. Add pudding mix and coconut; mix well. Fold in *1½ cups* whipped topping.

ARRANGE single layer of bananas on bottom of pie crust. Pour filling into crust. Top with *remaining* whipped topping. Refrigerate for 4 hours or until very set. Top with toasted or tinted coconut.   *Makes 8 servings*

Note: To make 2 pies, divide filling between 2 *prebaked* 9-inch (2-cup volume *each*) pie crusts. Top with *remaining* whipped topping.

PIES

Nestlé® Toll House® Chocolate Chip Pie

1 *unbaked* 9-inch (4-cup volume) deep-dish pie shell*
2 large eggs
½ cup all-purpose flour
½ cup granulated sugar
½ cup packed brown sugar
¾ cup (1½ sticks) butter, softened
1 cup (6 ounces) NESTLÉ TOLL HOUSE Semi-Sweet
    Chocolate Morsels
1 cup chopped nuts
    Sweetened whipped cream or ice cream (optional)

*If using frozen pie shell, use deep-dish style, thawed completely.
Bake on baking sheet; increase baking time slightly.*

PREHEAT oven to 325°F.

BEAT eggs in large mixer bowl on high speed until foamy. Beat in flour, granulated sugar and brown sugar. Beat in butter. Stir in morsels and nuts. Spoon into pie shell.

BAKE for 55 to 60 minutes or until knife inserted halfway between outside edge and center comes out clean. Cool on wire rack. Serve warm with whipped cream.

Makes 8 servings

PIES

Deep-Dish Peach Custard Pie

1 *unbaked* 9-inch (4-cup volume) deep-dish pie shell
3½ cups (about 7 medium) peeled, pitted and sliced
    peaches
1 can (14 ounces) NESTLÉ CARNATION Sweetened
    Condensed Milk
2 large eggs
¼ cup (½ stick) butter or margarine, melted
1 to 3 teaspoons lemon juice
½ teaspoon ground cinnamon
    Dash ground nutmeg
    Streusel Topping (recipe follows)

PREHEAT oven to 425°F.

ARRANGE peaches in pie shell. Combine sweetened condensed milk, eggs, butter, lemon juice, cinnamon and nutmeg in large mixer bowl; beat until smooth. Pour over peaches.

BAKE for 10 minutes. Sprinkle with Streusel Topping. Reduce oven temperature to 350°F.; bake for additional 55 to 60 minutes or until knife inserted near center comes out clean. Cool on wire rack. *Makes 8 servings*

Streusel Topping: COMBINE ⅓ cup all-purpose flour, ⅓ cup packed brown sugar and ⅓ cup chopped walnuts in medium bowl. Cut in 2 tablespoons butter or margarine with pastry blender or two knives until mixture resembles coarse crumbs.

PIES

Chocolate Mudslide Frozen Pie

1 *prepared* 9-inch (6 ounces) chocolate crumb crust
1 cup (6 ounces) NESTLÉ TOLL HOUSE Semi-Sweet
    Chocolate Morsels
1 teaspoon TASTER'S CHOICE 100% Pure Instant Coffee
1 teaspoon hot water
¾ cup sour cream
½ cup granulated sugar
1 teaspoon vanilla extract
1½ cups heavy whipping cream
1 cup powdered sugar
¼ cup NESTLÉ TOLL HOUSE Baking Cocoa
2 tablespoons NESTLÉ TOLL HOUSE Semi-Sweet Chocolate
    Mini Morsels

MELT *1 cup* morsels in small, *heavy-duty* saucepan over *lowest possible* heat. When morsels begin to melt, remove from heat; stir. Return to heat for a few seconds at a time, stirring until smooth. Remove from heat; cool for 10 minutes.

COMBINE Taster's Choice and water in medium bowl. Add sour cream, granulated sugar and vanilla extract; stir until sugar is dissolved. Stir in melted chocolate until smooth. Spread into crust; refrigerate.

BEAT cream, powdered sugar and cocoa in small mixer bowl until stiff peaks form. Spread or pipe over chocolate layer. Sprinkle with mini morsels. Freeze for at least 6 hours or until firm.   *Makes 8 servings*

PIES

Carnation® Key Lime Pie

1 *prepared* 9-inch (6 ounces) graham cracker crumb crust
1 can (14 ounces) NESTLÉ CARNATION Sweetened
  Condensed Milk
½ cup (about 3 medium limes) fresh lime juice
1 teaspoon grated lime peel
2 cups frozen whipped topping, thawed
  Lime peel twists or lime slices (optional)

BEAT sweetened condensed milk and lime juice in small mixer bowl until combined; stir in lime peel. Pour into crust; spread with whipped topping. Refrigerate for 2 hours or until set. Garnish with lime peel twists. *Makes 8 servings*

PIES

Chocolate Truffle Tart

Crust

⅔ cup all-purpose flour
½ cup powdered sugar
½ cup ground walnuts
6 tablespoons butter or margarine, softened
⅓ cup NESTLÉ TOLL HOUSE Baking Cocoa

Filling

1¼ cups heavy whipping cream
¼ cup granulated sugar
2 cups (12-ounce package) NESTLÉ TOLL HOUSE
    Semi-Sweet Chocolate Morsels
2 tablespoons seedless raspberry jam
    Sweetened whipped cream (optional)
    Fresh raspberries (optional)

PREHEAT oven to 350°F.

For Crust

BEAT flour, powdered sugar, nuts, butter and cocoa in large mixer bowl until soft dough forms. Press dough onto bottom and up side of ungreased 9- or 9½-inch fluted tart pan with removable bottom or 9-inch pie plate.

BAKE for 12 to 14 minutes or until puffed. Cool completely in pan on wire rack.

For Filling

BRING cream and granulated sugar in medium saucepan *just to a boil*, stirring occasionally. Remove from heat. Stir in morsels and jam; let stand for 5 minutes. Whisk until smooth. Transfer to small mixer bowl. Cover; refrigerate for 45 to 60 minutes or until mixture is cooled and slightly thickened.

BEAT for 20 to 30 seconds or just until color lightens slightly. Spoon into crust. Refrigerate until firm. Remove side of pan; garnish with whipped cream and raspberries.

Makes 8 servings

PIES

Libby's® Famous Pumpkin Pie

1 *unbaked* 9-inch (4-cup volume) deep-dish pie shell
¾ cup granulated sugar
1 teaspoon ground cinnamon
½ teaspoon salt
½ teaspoon ground ginger
¼ teaspoon ground cloves
2 large eggs
1 can (15 ounces) LIBBY'S 100% Pure Pumpkin
1 can (12 fluid ounces) NESTLÉ CARNATION
   Evaporated Milk
Whipped cream

MIX sugar, cinnamon, salt, ginger and cloves in small bowl. Beat eggs in large bowl. Stir in pumpkin and sugar-spice mixture. Gradually stir in evaporated milk.

POUR into pie shell.

BAKE in preheated 425°F. oven for 15 minutes. Reduce temperature to 350°F.; bake for 40 to 50 minutes or until knife inserted near center comes out clean. Cool on wire rack for 2 hours. Serve immediately or refrigerate. Top with whipped cream before serving.   *Makes 8 servings*

Note: Do not freeze. (The crust will separate from the filling).

Tip: 1¾ teaspoons pumpkin pie spice may be substituted for the cinnamon, ginger and cloves, but the taste will be slightly different.

For 2 shallow pies: Substitute two 9-inch (2-cup volume) pie shells. Bake in preheated 425°F. oven for 15 minutes. Reduce temperature to 350°F.; bake for 20 to 30 minutes or until pies test done.

PIES

Quick Tiramisu

1 package (18 ounces) NESTLÉ TOLL HOUSE
    Refrigerated Sugar Cookie Bar Dough
1 package (8 ounces) ⅓ less fat cream cheese
½ cup granulated sugar
¾ teaspoon TASTER'S CHOICE 100% Pure Instant Coffee
    dissolved in ¾ cup cold water, *divided*
1 container (8 ounces) frozen whipped topping, thawed
1 tablespoon NESTLÉ TOLL HOUSE Baking Cocoa

PREHEAT oven to 325°F.

DIVIDE cookie dough into 20 pieces. Shape into 2½×1-inch oblong shapes. Place on ungreased baking sheets.

BAKE for 10 to 12 minutes or until light golden brown around edges. Cool on baking sheets for 1 minute; remove to wire racks to cool completely.

BEAT cream cheese and sugar in large mixer bowl until smooth. Beat in ¼ *cup* Taster's Choice. Fold in whipped topping. Layer 6 cookies in 8-inch-square baking dish. Sprinkle each cookie with *1 teaspoon* Taster's Choice. Spread *one-third* cream cheese mixture over cookies. Repeat layers 2 more times with *12* cookies, *remaining* coffee and *remaining* cream cheese mixture. Cover; refrigerate for 2 to 3 hours. Crumble *remaining* cookies over top. Sift cocoa over cookies. Cut into squares.

Makes 6 to 8 servings

DESSERTS & MORE

41

Petit Pain au Chocolate

1 package (17.25 ounces) frozen puff pastry sheets, thawed
1 cup (6 ounces) NESTLÉ TOLL HOUSE Milk Chocolate Morsels, *divided*
1 large egg, beaten
1 bar (2 ounces *total*) NESTLÉ TOLL HOUSE Semi-Sweet Chocolate Baking Bars, broken into pieces
2 tablespoons butter or margarine
1 cup powdered sugar
2 tablespoons hot water

PREHEAT oven to 350°F. Grease 2 baking sheets.

UNFOLD *1* pastry sheet on lightly floured surface. Roll out to make 10-inch square. Cut into 4 squares. Place *2 tablespoons* morsels in center of each square. Brush edges lightly with beaten egg and fold squares to form triangles. Press edges to seal. Place on prepared baking sheet about 2 inches apart. Repeat with *remaining* pastry sheet. Brush top of each pastry with beaten egg.

BAKE for 15 to 17 minutes or until puffed and golden. Cool on baking sheets for 2 minutes; remove to wire racks to cool completely.

MELT baking bar and butter in small, uncovered, microwave-safe bowl on HIGH (100%) power for 30 seconds. STIR. Bar may retain some of its original shape. If necessary, microwave at additional 10- to 15-second intervals, stirring just until bar is melted. Stir in sugar. Add water, stirring until icing is smooth, adding additional water, if necessary. Drizzle icing over pastries.

Makes 8 pastries

DESSERTS & MORE

Toll House® Famous Fudge

1½ cups granulated sugar
⅔ cup (5-fluid-ounce can) NESTLÉ CARNATION Evaporated Milk
2 tablespoons butter or margarine
¼ teaspoon salt
2 cups miniature marshmallows
1½ cups (9 ounces) NESTLÉ TOLL HOUSE Semi-Sweet Chocolate Morsels
½ cup chopped pecans or walnuts (optional)
1 teaspoon vanilla extract

LINE 8-inch square baking pan with foil.

COMBINE sugar, evaporated milk, butter and salt in medium, *heavy-duty* saucepan. Bring to a *full rolling boil* over medium heat, stirring constantly. Boil, stirring constantly, for 4 to 5 minutes. Remove from heat.

STIR in marshmallows, morsels, nuts and vanilla extract. Stir vigorously for 1 minute or until marshmallows are melted. Pour into prepared baking pan; refrigerate for 2 hours or until firm. Lift from pan; remove foil. Cut into pieces.   *Makes 49 pieces*

For Milk Chocolate Fudge: SUBSTITUTE 1¾ cups (11.5-ounce package) NESTLÉ TOLL HOUSE Milk Chocolate Morsels for Semi-Sweet Morsels.

For Butterscotch Fudge: SUBSTITUTE 1⅔ cups (11-ounce package) NESTLÉ TOLL HOUSE Butterscotch Flavored Morsels for Semi-Sweet Morsels.

DESSERTS & MORE

43

Chocolate Mint Truffles

1¾ cups (11.5-ounce package) NESTLÉ TOLL HOUSE
 Milk Chocolate Morsels
1 cup (6 ounces) NESTLÉ TOLL HOUSE Semi-Sweet
 Chocolate Morsels
¾ cup heavy whipping cream
1 tablespoon peppermint extract
1½ cups finely chopped walnuts, toasted, or
 NESTLÉ TOLL HOUSE Baking Cocoa

LINE baking sheet with wax paper.

PLACE milk chocolate and semi-sweet morsels in large mixer
bowl. Heat cream to a gentle boil in small saucepan; pour over
morsels. Let stand for 1 minute; stir until smooth. Stir in
peppermint extract. Cover with plastic wrap; refrigerate for
35 to 45 minutes or until slightly thickened. Stir just until
color lightens slightly. (*Do not* overmix or truffles will be grainy.)

DROP by rounded teaspoonful onto prepared baking sheet;
refrigerate for 10 to 15 minutes. Shape into balls; roll in walnuts
or cocoa. Store in airtight container in refrigerator.

Makes about 48 truffles

Variation: After rolling chocolate mixture into balls, freeze for
30 to 40 minutes. Microwave 1¾ cups (11.5-ounce package)
NESTLÉ TOLL HOUSE Milk Chocolate Morsels and
3 tablespoons vegetable shortening in medium, uncovered,
microwave-safe bowl on MEDIUM-HIGH (70%) power for
1 minute. STIR. Morsels may retain some of their original
shape. If necessary, microwave at additional 10- to 15-second
intervals, stirring just until morsels are melted. Dip truffles into
chocolate mixture; shake off excess. Place on foil-lined baking
sheets. Refrigerate for 15 to 20 minutes or until set. Store in
airtight container in refrigerator.

**DESSERTS
& MORE**

44

Rich Chocolate Mousse

1 cup (6 ounces) NESTLÉ TOLL HOUSE Semi-Sweet
    Chocolate Morsels
3 tablespoons butter, cut into pieces
2 teaspoons TASTER'S CHOICE 100% Pure Instant Coffee
1 tablespoon hot water
2 teaspoons vanilla extract
½ cup heavy whipping cream

MICROWAVE morsels and butter in medium, uncovered,
microwave-safe bowl on HIGH (100%) power for 1 minute.
STIR. Morsels may retain some of their original shape. If
necessary, microwave at additional 10- to 15-second intervals,
stirring just until morsels are melted. Dissolve Taster's Choice
in hot water; stir into chocolate. Stir in vanilla extract; cool to
room temperature.

WHIP cream in small mixer bowl on high speed until stiff
peaks form; fold into chocolate mixture. Spoon into tall
glasses; refrigerate for 1 hour or until set. Garnish as desired.

Makes 2 servings

**DESSERTS
& MORE**

45

Holiday Peppermint Bark

**2 cups (12-ounce package) NESTLÉ TOLL HOUSE
Premier White Morsels
24 hard peppermint candies, unwrapped**

LINE baking sheet with wax paper.

MICROWAVE morsels in medium, uncovered, microwave-safe bowl on MEDIUM-HIGH (70%) power for 1 minute. STIR. Morsels may retain some of their original shape. If necessary, microwave at additional 10- to 15-second intervals, stirring just until morsels are melted.

PLACE peppermint candies in *heavy-duty* resealable plastic food storage bag. Crush candies using rolling pin or other heavy object. While holding strainer over melted morsels, pour crushed candy into strainer. Shake to release all small candy pieces; reserve larger candy pieces. Stir morsel-peppermint mixture.

SPREAD mixture to desired thickness on prepared baking sheet. Sprinkle with reserved candy pieces; press in lightly. Let stand for about 1 hour or until firm. Break into pieces. Store in airtight container at room temperature.

Makes about 1 pound candy

**DESSERTS
& MORE**